WILD CREATURE

Joan Margarit (1938-2021) was born in Sanaüja, La Segarra region, in Catalonia. He was an architect as well as a poet, and from 1968 until his retirement was also Professor of Structural Calculations at Barcelona's Technical School of Architecture, working for part of that time on Gaudí's Sagrada Família cathedral. He first published poetry in Spanish, but after four books decided to write in Catalan. From 1980 he began to establish his reputation as a major Catalan poet. As well as publishing many collections in Catalan, he published Spanish versions of all his work, gaining recognition as a leading poet in Spanish.

In 2008 he received the Premio Nacional de Poesía del Estado Español for his collection *Casa de Misericòrdia*, as well as the Premi Nacional de Literatura de la Generalitat de Catalunya. In 2013 he was awarded Mexico's Premio de Poetas del Mundo Latino Víctor Sandoval for all his poetry. He was awarded the 2019 Cervantes Prize, the Spanish-speaking world's highest literary honour, which generally alternates between Spanish and Latin American writers, receiving this from King Felipe VI of Spain at a special ceremony at Barcelona's Palauet Albéniz in December 2020, the presentation being delayed by the coronavirus pandemic. He also received the Reina Sofía Prize for Ibero-American Poetry 2019, the most important poetry award for Spain, Portugal and Latin America.

Tugs in the Fog: Selected Poems (Bloodaxe Books, 2006), translated by Anna Crowe, the first English translation of his Catalan poetry, was a Poetry Book Society Recommended Translation. *Strangely Happy*, later poems from *Casa de Misericòrdia* (2007) and *Misteriosament feliç* (2008), also translated by Anna Crowe, was published by Bloodaxe in 2011. A third translation by Anna Crowe, *Love Is a Place* (Bloodaxe Books, 2016) includes all the poems from three recent Catalan collections: *No era lluny ni difícil* (It Wasn't Far Away or Difficult, 2010), *Es perd el senyal* (The Signal Is Fading, 2012) and *Estimar és un lloc* (From Where to Begin to Love Again, 2014). His final collection *Wild Creature* (Bloodaxe Books, 2021), also translated by Anna Crowe, brings together poems from his two last two collections, *Un hivern fascinant* (An amazing winter, 2017) and *Animal de bosc* (Wild creature, 2020).

JOAN MARGARIT

Wild Creature

TRANSLATED BY
ANNA CROWE

BLOODAXE BOOKS

ISBN: 978 1 78037 592 2

First published 2021 by
Bloodaxe Books Ltd,
Eastburn,
South Park,
Hexham,
Northumberland NE46 1BS.

www.bloodaxebooks.com
For further information about Bloodaxe titles
please visit our website and join our mailing list
or write to the above address for a catalogue

Supported using public funding by
**ARTS COUNCIL
ENGLAND**

Cover design: Neil Astley & Pamela Robertson-Pearce.

Printed in Great Britain by Bell & Bain Limited, Glasgow, Scotland, on
acid-free paper sourced from mills with FSC chain of custody certification.

ACKNOWLEDGEMENTS

Wild Creature is a translation by Anna Crowe of Joan Margarit's final two Catalan collections *Un hivern fascinant* (An amazing winter, 2017) and *Animal de bosc* (Wild creature, 2020), both published by Edicions Proa Grup62, Barcelona. The translation of this work was supported by a grant from Instituto Cervantes.

**Instituto
Cervantes**

CONTENTS

WILD CREATURE (2020)

An amazing winter

(2017)

An amazing winter

The poppies are disappearing,
wiped out like the weeds.
Very soon, the wind's red brushstrokes
will no longer blow through fields of wheat.
Who will be able to make sense, one day,
of Van Gogh's paintings?
The world I live in is still familiar,
though subtle changes already alert me:
it won't go back to being mine.
It's not about it being a hell: it can be understood.
Oblivion comes, reassuring us.
And happiness, happiness always returns.

Atocha Hill

Our paths cross. The two of them going up:
the wheelchair in which, huddled
and moaning, a young man sits,
and the father, who is pushing him.
To gain more power, he throws his feet backwards
and stretches out arms and legs as far as he can.
Like this, bent double and tense,
he can barely manage the climb.
I know what he feels: that he is getting old.
For one accursed moment, in pitying this father,
I am mistaken: he still has his child.

Now that they have passed,
I smile at them as they move into the distance.
A woman glares at me from her doorway.
She doesn't know what love scene she is witnessing.

The mysterious island

I arrived there as an adolescent,
finding it a kindly, utterly beautiful place.
And it was my home.
Speaking Castilian, I did my best
to speak it with the same melodiousness.

I lived in a city where women, opening
their windows, would place cushions on the sills
to rest their arms on. The streets
with houses of pink stucco dropped down to the port.

One day I went back to my harsh country,
but the island is close, in my memory.
I will never be able to disembark there again.
Tenerife, the fifties:
a place and a time. The only ones
I would like to return to. Through its warm sea
a shark was already swimming: my future.

Works of love

The motive doesn't matter.
We have to search among the remains for what has survived.
Might we not feel ourselves insecure
if our feelings
were frontier lands
lost, regained, lost once more?
For loving is not falling in love.
It is going on building, time and again,
the same courtyard in which to listen to the blackbirds
in springtime when it's still dark.
It is the only birdsong that could be Schubert.
You and I as in our twenties, alone in the kitchen,
we grow strong listening to that melody.
We have never had so much light as now.

Woman about to do her hands

She puts her fingers in the water
and thinks of the caresses they have made.
But the water slowly cools,
as do the words
that sheltered her and have left her alone.

Interest in life ends much sooner
than the young suppose.

Everything cools, and we need
the weariness of having loved.
In order to desire what is approaching.
So different.

Building a destiny

In the woods at night,
around the camp-fire, we boys used to sing
The wind will bring our cry to where you are.
Afterwards we would fall sleep in the tent,
under the white canvas, while gazing at the shadows
that the pine branches were drawing there.

It took me a few more years
to discover the ancient Taoist poets,
those who would teach me the meaning
of silence and the moon.
Now solitude is laying itself down
over the words.
The wind will bring our cry to where you are.
You will hear it. And there will be no one.

Verdaguer

Abandoned and alone, in this room
that today is a museum, he lay dying.
At the same time in the same bed
we Catalan poets were being born
while a great crowd was filling the streets
and bidding him farewell. Catholic piety
and a decadent mythology
served as a skeleton to a goodness
and compassion like those of my own home:
rural and violent. Verdaguer is the oak tree
that we have always needed in this country of ours:
first we set it on fire, then, at once,
we mourn it for years on end. Burning and weeping.
The desolation of malice.
I love him like a son. And he is my father.

Familiarities

I remember him when I see freezing fog
wrapping itself around a building under construction.
He was a good architect whom the two factions
had obliged to bow his head.
We got along well.
Until I turned into a young man
and he began little by little to confuse
architecture with the squalor
of the places where he sometimes had to search for it.
With no one around, the construction work goes on in the fog.
It moves me to sense his cowardice in myself.

Goyescas

Weep, weep, but listen to Granados.
What can the *Goyescas* say,
if what Goya painted best was death?
The success in New York, and the White House.
The premonition of his fear of the sea.
Listening to Granados, everything makes you shiver.
The *Sussex* has weighed anchor to cross the Channel:
the old, dilapidated ferry
will be a terror of iron, like that of the man
in the white shirt in the *Executions of the Third of May*.
One horror inside another: the war in the sea.
Granados's wife is swimming in the waves
and he dives in to save her.
But he clings to her, unable to swim.
Whenever the last Goyesca is being played –
the 'Song of love and death' –
they drown again. Their arms around each other.

On insults

> All conditionings tend to result in people loving their
> inevitable social destiny.
>
> ALDOUS HUXLEY, *A happy world*

The young go by
in ripped jeans, showing their knees.
Older men and women also wear them.
They are the fashion and are displayed in shop windows.
I belong to another era
where this torn elegance
would have been appalling. Like spitting on the poor.
We are on another road. Towards another poverty.
I cannot give up on good sense:
maybe life has to rip everything up
and life itself is an enormous rent.
But if that were so,
we need not have built the cathedrals.
Nor was crime necessary. With love we have enough.

Memory's punishment

We used to come, cutting across the cruelty
of the summer drought, a kind of homeland.
At Tàrrega we entered by a road
where the first thing we saw was the elm:
facing the swimming-pools, like the character
in a fairy-tale, its shade protected us.
And the knowledge that, in the water, Joana
could swim freely like the other girls.

They closed the pools and the elm died.
The dry stump, its three boughs lopped, remained.
The silent song of hundreds of birds,
of the wind murmuring among leaves,
of the echoing voices from those happy days.
The indignity of exaggerating memories.

North wind

(October 2017)

Clear as glass it howls from one beach to the next
with their hard, smooth stones.
It makes the sea shine, this furious broom.
It seeks us out, we know each other. It was her wind.
The blues of the sea and the sky seem to be
the sumptuous remains of some mythology.
Plunging into clean and freezing water
brings to mind the sudden violence
life often has.

I gaze at this little port where there are no longer
any boats or sailing-yachts. In autumn they leave,
seeking moorings that may be more safe.
The dull, insistent noise of the waves
and the untuned violin
that the gusts are playing
are the mysterious reply from the future.
For the first time I listen to it and trust it.
It speaks of you and me. And of a port that's safe
now that no sailing-yachts or boats remain.

Our time

When we became aware of it, it was already at the windows.
As though it had to stay. But now
the only thing shedding light on us is this vague fog.
A light that wounds, sometimes.
Ours was a more innocent time:
on the building-sites we had a party, to celebrate
that no one got hurt, that the structure
reached the top floor, and the roof was on.
We lived in streets well suited
to names like *of the Camelias*.
At night, among the terrace roofs, we lit the lamps
in the attic of our young days.
Among the gentle, distant voices,
sometimes there rises up a cry of terror.
But a wound is also somewhere to live.

Where do we come from? What are we?
Where are we going?

(Paul Gauguin, Tahiti, 1898)

Pinned to the wall – four drawing-pins –
the print of the painting
I had in my room when a student.
It was the middle double-page spread from a magazine
that was badly produced, while it left on my gaze
some powerful and difficult truth.

Sixty years have passed, and now, one morning,
visiting the Fine Arts Museum in Boston,
I have entered the dimness
of a room where the spotlights are trained
on a single enormous painting.
It speaks to me only of *What are we?*
This final what am I, is the only reward
and the only punishment. That poor print
could tell me none of this. Nor would I have understood it.
I am here giving thanks that I am being sent,
from so long ago and with no fuss,
the powerful peace
which protected me in my youth.

All-in wrestling

When I was a child, my father used to take me to it.
The four-sided space made of white canvas
with railings made of ropes, the brightly-lit ring,
was in the middle of enormous darkness.
When the two wrestlers appeared,
the one that the crowd already hated
was the one we knew would lose.

Time and again, the loser kept falling
on to the canvas, pushing himself up again
like people who wept for their dead.

He would end by being hurled over the ropes
into the dismal region where the spectators sat,
where his schoolmasters had been purged or shot.

There I learned more than in the classroom.
What wrestling – *free fighting* – means. The meaning of *free*.
They closed the premises. They always close them.
But the crowd is already yelling elsewhere.

Stroke

He concentrates his mind on the unmoving hand
to force it to make a fist, a gesture
as though to win back a lost friendship.
In hospital he does everything they tell him,
but that is not obeying, only remaining distant.
Clinging to the bars,
he throws his left leg forwards
with a dry sound like the crack of a whip.
His strength progresses with no date,
between two worn parallel lines
like a single note on a stave.
We know our certainties so well
that we've already sworn not to speak of it.
Lying in his room in the half-light,
he fiddles clumsily with a small radio.
Music penetrates
even in the destruction. Silence in the corridor:
suddenly a cry of anguish.
The past has lost its power to move.

Future

It's the same house, the same courtyard.
And the turtle-dove in the cypress
is as real as it was so many years ago.
I have opened a box and out came
her gold bracelets: some very, very slender
rings her arm slipped through.
The true tragedy has begun.
When I can no longer admit any lie
and when the truth is no more than the ash
of some simple desire from when she lived.
It's the same house, the same courtyard.
All that has changed is the depth of shadow
that death casts on the marble table.
In the small hours, quantum mechanics
is a silent Homer: it is composing its *Iliad*.

The albatross

Motionless and suspended between two air-currents
there is a seagull keeping watch over the beach.
I remember Baudelaire, and when I read
that poem of his for the first time.
I have never seen an albatross.
I began, as all do, by wanting to be someone else.
My youth was receding behind me
before I realised
that it wouldn't be the wings of a giant
that would prevent me from walking.
That the poet has his own mirror
before which everything passes slowly
and where those poems he will never write
try out their majestic flight.
But they are in reality behind,
where the real world goes furiously by.
Difficult, impossible at times,
they are for ever passing – they never stop –
at a terrifying speed.

Road

Narrow and with the asphalt of many years ago:
overlooking the knives of dark rocks,
one bend after another above the sea.
And now they have made a tunnel that crosses the past.
But no new road can bring me
to the brightest place of all, that nothing sullies
nor makes hope fall apart.

The old road slowly follows the sea.
At its foot there is the limpid water that once
was that of our children.

We are this road, you and I.
Neither of us will know it but, soon,
on the horizon we will be for ever home.

Through pain

I've never forgotten the blow to the back of my head from
    a guardia civil
who told me loudly and harshly: *Speak a Christian tongue, boy!*
Until I was in my forties, the police
would conduct their questioning using torture.
Only in Castilian.

But through so many humiliations
before the words something else reached me.
Gentle and indestructible.
As clear as nothing else would ever be.
It came from a place that I think is childhood.
Sometimes I feel it mixed with music,
like ten or fifteen notes that suddenly move me,
but I don't know why or since when.
As though it were a tomb with no name
to which for love's sake I have always brought roses.

It is the strength and light of something unknown to me.
It warns me, protects me from a place that I do not love.
From a pointless rancour. From myself. From others.
From some dangerous indifference.
It is in my poems.
For that reason, too, I have written them in Castilian.

What enlightens me

When I was twenty I went inside Altamira on my own.
The faint reddish light
was like the reflection from a fire
in the rock of the low, overhanging roof.
The loneliness of those strange Picassos
I had to keep inside me
because I was still too young.
At every age something is held back
that has not been understood:
the cold walls of a Romanesque church,
the order composed by Kant, Hegel and Nietzsche.
I have no more ages left.
And besides, this present, for when should I save it?
But now I can enter a huge cave
where all the museums of the world already fit.
At the back I hear the hoarse voice
of the remote, beloved animal
from which, so slowly, we have been coming.
Crime and philosophy were already in the eyes
of that prehistoric Gauguin when, humbly,
he painted by the light of the fire.

More than a song

It was like a spell.
I've always sung it to myself, I'm humming it still.
I heard it for the first time
from the top of a cart going along a road full of pot-holes.
A woman's voice was singing softly
in the ancient rhythm of her forebears:
'My shepherd and I,
oh we lived upon sweet nothings.
My shepherd and I
oh we lived on love alone.'
One note per syllable, in a soft voice.
The people who looked after me when I was small
and the frozen mud of the wheel-ruts.
That pure cold of the air in the unwatered farmland
the same that comes to me from understanding.
This is what I am: a people with no name.

Thermopylae

It was two and a half thousand years ago. Defending a pass
they died for freedom.
No other myth is as moving.
It consoled us when we were young.
You search for a place where you may become strong,
and you forget that the traitor is yourself.
But the triumph of the myth is you and me:
the young man and young woman died
so that we two old ones might become free.

Life

I have trodden it the way old sailors ploughed the sea,
and I have let myself be guided by different stars.
I remember a city. In the port at night,
when we looked up,
the sky resembled a flag
huge with stars.

Desperately, I strive that nothing
I have loved should be lost. And that the end,
just before it turns to darkness,
may be the supernova of understanding.

Golden Age

Literature that takes me back to Franco-ism:
to those utterly tedious *poemas pastoriles*,
vanity, anger. To the revering of a sarcasm
and an often ecclesiastical savagery.
I ended up mistrusting wit forever.
Even the Quixote became part
of having lost the war. The threat
of literature that was used,
by dint of contempt, to steal my childhood.
All at once, the classics go quiet.
Silently, structural calculations
rescued my struggle to unite
reason and happiness. I'm not talking about hope:
today all that matters is that the child
no longer has to beg ever again for forgiveness
from those two sinister faces of the poets
whom Velázquez painted.

'two sinister faces': these are the Spanish Golden Age poets and
lifelong bitter rivals, Luís de Góngora and Francisco de Quevedo.

Rides

The time for loving
is that of the pace of the seasons.
The time for sex is the present moment.
Sex is a horse without a rider,
we all have to leap on to its back.
Hearing that violent neighing,
we went to mount it, you and I each alone.
To ride our own desperation.
It terrified us that fate might come
and we'd not recognise it.
We were searching for the very thing we were fleeing.
Galloping, getting further away from each other,
we came to a place we weren't expecting:
the peaceful half-light of a stable
where the hooves no longer thud against the door.
He too has become old. We mount and ride,
while knowing we don't need to reach any place.
And that it's the same horse that now carries us,
at that pace, towards death.

Photograph of a girl

Beside the hearth, where the fire is still burning,
she leaves the doll on the floor and yawns sleepily.
It is so long ago: now, *long ago* means
I now have no strength left.

But I smile imagining that one day
I shall think I mustn't forget
the doll when it's time to tuck her up in bed.
That later I shall go round switching off the lights
because the house will already be quiet.
And that then, at last, I shall be happy.

De senectute

When we are young, love
takes no account of forgetting.
The future is in charge, even though it shines
like a mere puddle at the back of the brain.
Pain imposes order, rings out like a warning:
it's the hooter on the tug
that drags us out of the harbour.

We pay dearly for trying to destroy pain
because love too is there.
Wisdom lies in rescuing all of it.
Let our eyes display, watchful,
their splendid uselessness.
Without pain
we would never have been able to love like this.

Jorge Manrique

Surrounded by his wife
and by his children and brothers
and servants.

This voice, respectful and grave,
has the face of some truth or other
in the shape of a lie. It upsets us
like a fly devouring the spider.
These are not the commonplaces about death,
but a magnificent future of vast indifference:
this is the subject of the one hundred iron lines
rising out of the rhetorical swamp of the *Coplas*.
And suddenly, that truth
slamming the door leaves me on my own.
Alone with my death. Without disappointment.

If you read this book

A few centuries from now, these lines
will sound old-fashioned to you.
It's fugacity, a word
that implies both delicacy,
desolation and indifference.
But it's nothing more than a point in the universe
making ready to leave silently
at the speed of light: fugacity
is simply that.
Calling it hope is comforting.

Time's lyric

The mind is an artist.
Memories are its complete works.
Death burns this work.
But someone like Cavafy or Neruda –
certain poets – rescue it in their lines.

The poem and time are today bound together
by an amazing winter into which you disappear
like a bee inside a flower.
Time pushes in gusts.
This is the strongest. The least lyrical.

Courage

The war has ended. Peace doesn't come.
Rough and silent, evening falls.
I am four, I watch how my grandmother pisses
standing up straight beside a road,
opening her legs wide beneath her skirts.
Every time I remember it, I hear
that stream falling noisily on the ground.
It was that woman who taught me
that love is toughness and clarity,
and that without courage you cannot love.
This was not literature: she couldn't read.

Final performances

When I was young I was Macbeth.
The play was staged among pillars
of reinforced concrete. Beneath iron girders.
I declaimed: 'My kingdom is laid waste.'
I betrayed through vengeance.
Sex was a weapon with a bad blade:
it made ugly wounds.
At that time there was some fog
because of which, or for the sake of which, to die.
It is night: dawn is a long time coming.
The voice of Lady Macbeth, brusque and pragmatic, tells me,
'What's done cannot be undone.'

Known cruelty

(17 August 2017)

The same city only lasts its span of time.
All Barcelonas lie one inside another
like invisible Russian dolls.

The city that I love had few lamps burning
in the impoverished nights of an infamous country.
Now it's another Barcelona.

Maybe today, if it weren't for so many memories,
I wouldn't now love it.
Suddenly nothing comes to an end.
As a child I saw murderers at mass:
the same silences, flowers, candles
for the same crimes.

Purposes

For good. For evil.
What had to be my misfortune
was the strongest pain
and love of my life.
Life at times is a cruise-ship,
which, illuminated, sails nowhere
with this enormous hull
made of the hollow iron of purpose.
Sometimes life is nothing more
than the simplest flower, the one growing
beside every road.
Forgetting can never make me innocent.
Ignorance always makes me guilty.

Behind the glass

Leaving is this passion
that comes late. That can be violent.
We are part of some music. It changes,
and you must know how to listen to where it is carrying you.
Sometimes it's mysteriously apt.
But now it's a difficult music.
Abstract and discordant, it impels me to leave:
it is hope's final seduction.
Deaf Beethoven helps me reject it.
Because the present still lights up
like a huge diamond of time
where I am no longer.
It is from here that I love you, because look:
I shall leave while loving. I have nothing else.
I am that gaze behind the glass.

Instants

Cadolles, someone says: a word
I haven't heard for sixty years.
It's the word for those pools
that the sea, as it retreats, leaves around the rocks.
What the sea has forgotten. Lost words.
The desolate instant
from when you were a boy and had finished
the last page of *Treasure Island*.
The moment just before beginning a poem.
And even *the instant*:
the first that, when it comes, will be after you.

Mythology

Abstract things that will destroy us
like absolute zero or the speed
of light. There was never any point
in imagining that these things were
enormous powers of volition to appeal to.
With a certain air of mythology
there remains the strength of love,
powerful as gravity,
silent and motherly as gravity is:
it can bring warmth to the moon –
a frozen rock –
if we are thinking of someone when we gaze at it.

The solitude of the sea

The vessel sails back to the same island.
I think of Juan Ramón: everything is ready
for eternity. I have taken another step
towards the interior of the age I shall neither
be able to judge nor remember.
For some time I've stopped reading, nor will I go back to,
the tired poets who stopped writing,
Gil de Biedma or Rimbaud, for example.
For me the only thing that counts now
is what has been sought after until death.
The amazing winter of the animal deep down.

'Juan Ramón': Juan Ramón Jimenez, who went into exile in the
US after Franco won the Spanish Civil War, but who went on
writing about his native Moguer in Andalucía, while working in
Washington DC. He published in 1949 a collection called *El
Animal de Fondo* (The animal deep down).

No other beginning

I came to be able to hear a wolf
howling in the depths of a forest.
And the quail calling to each other hidden in the wheat.
I encountered at night the eyes of foxes.
I have seen huge vultures above a sea of mist.
But nothing has ended, and I'm not aware of any loss.
What was it I possessed?
I can't play with fear as I did when a child.
I am in the depths of the forest of all the fairy-tales,
smiling and happy not to be young.
Knowing that once it has opened,
a crack never closes up again.

Epilogue to *An amazing winter*

The two mysteries of *before* and *after*, creating a tension that puts its stamp on thought, now have me balanced in a new kind of lightness. What I have always called and imagined to be *the future* has been supplanted by forgetting it and, at the same time, my past has been catapulted so far away that now it too is barely more than oblivion. It is a new equilibrium. The remaining imminence of stability or the final disorder.

That may have had an influence on these poems, since poetry is written only from inside the poet, but it has not caused my voice to change, because a single life does not allow for more than one voice. I have never taken seriously the question of heteronyms. One's own voice – even that which we call, in the deepest sense, style – is not chosen, it forms part of what we strictly are. Every poet reaches it while searching deep inside him/herself for the basic material, surely created during childhood and thereafter hidden – sometimes forever – during adolescence and early youth, on top of which life goes piling up, moreover, the long apprenticeship of the use of commonplaces.

I began writing poems at the beginning of the second half of the 20th century, when poets like Pablo Neruda, Rafael Alberti, Salvador Espriu, Gabriel Ferrater or Joan Vinyoli were still building their poetic works. I waited for the publication of their books with even greater fervour because of the difficulties there were in buying them during Franco-ism. Poets such as that same Pablo Neruda, Gabriel Celaya or Blas de Otero declared that theirs was a trade like that of the blacksmith or miner, with serious social obligations for what was said and how it was said. Juan Ramón Jiménez, Carles Riba or Josep Carner spoke to us about a poetry that was everlasting and at the margin, or fairly at the margin, of any pressure, especially ideological pressure, that did not come from the poet's own life. It is worth saying that what they all, in fact, dedicated themselves to was writing good poems, and that each one of them, when defending how poetry should be written, did no more than voice an apologia for the only way he knew how or was able to write it.

The poems in this book are written from this side of the 21st century. The notable changes that have come about in our complex society offer nothing new to man or woman in their existential solitude, unless it is to make this more pronounced. Where we are still capable of making a difference is in superficial matters. But the question, from the point of view of poetry, is still, it seems to me, knowing where the depths lie or, to phrase it differently, where the surface ends.

I recall another time this question arose, in a discussion I had with the most *trendy* students during one of my classes on Structural Calculations in the 1970s at the School of Architecture in Barcelona. They defended the freedom of anyone claiming to be a good architect to believe in anything, that the earth was flat, for example. Or the freedom to believe that one could be a good painter in spite of not being able to paint a portrait. For me, who believed – and still believe – the complete opposite, what happens is that, when facility goes in the same direction as my desires, I have the feeling that I must be in the wrong.

In fact it was already about the problem of the loss of the weight of humility and honesty – each one of us does and talks about what he knows – together with an idealisation, therefore another falsity, of the importance of one's own desire. Assuredly a large part of the art and politics of today turns on these questions.

I think of Juan Ramón or Neruda in the second half of the 20th century and, for example, of Francisco Brines or myself today, and also of those a little younger than us, like Luis García Montero, or much younger, like Manuel Forcano, Raquel Lanseros or Josep M. Rodríguez, and I don't see that there has occurred anything fundamentally new in the relation that the poet has with the poem. I see the writing of poetry during these years as opening a tunnel from 1955 to today passing beneath the mountain of lives and events, which have brought all their repercussions – seismic movements, filterings, echoes, etc – to the poems, and which never cease, whatever may be happening on the surface. The poet, the artist, the musician is someone who has the good fortune – or the bad luck – to live at one and the same time on the surface and below the groundwater level of life.

One of the two main strengths of poetry is its truth, whether it is a realistic poem, surrealist, explicit, cryptic or whatever type by which the studious classify our ways of writing them. But the reality is that a good poem is such a difficult thing to make, and it is so unlikely that one may manage to write it, that these classifications are always a posteriori, since the poem, in spite of the many previous intentions and positions it may have held, is built, to put it plainly and bluntly, more as it can be than as one may wish. Without scholarship there would still continue to be poetry. But without truth, not.

The other important strength of poetry is beauty. Truth and beauty may be superimposed, but the truth often lies in places where beauty has no part to play. The territory of art is simply where they come together. The poet has to know that there is no place that must not be explored, because beauty can be all around, though hidden or scarcely obvious in the majority of cases. The worst mistake a poet can make is to think that, in coming across only beauty or only truth, he already has both things, and can now write the poem, because behind one of them there has to be the other. Inspiration is, precisely, that rare and difficult event that consists in finding a place where it is fairly probable that there may be found together, inseparable, truth and beauty.

But the poems have to open a path through the lives of those who read them, amongst a mountain of important or trivial things which often set in motion mechanisms of survival which, in an imperious fashion, impose deceit. The need for prestige, for example, from or through the ambiguous and dangerous word *love*. Or through another word, likewise ambiguous but, more than dangerous, presumptuous: *friendship*. A large number of the deceits which claim to resolve the simple fear of loneliness grow in the shelter of these two words, which can be two poisonous snakes in the jungle of the dictionary. But lying, broadly speaking, always poses more serious problems than those it attempts to solve.

This is why, sooner or later, we have urgent need of some tool that is incompatible with lying. Poetry is one of the most powerful. Truth and beauty together. They are not always so. When they are it is more to do with love. Then, yes.

Wild creature

(2020)

The two snowfalls

Seeing so much snow falling everywhere,
you and I have remembered, without leaving the house,
the snow in which we found our love.
We hadn't known each other very long
and we spent that day until well into the small hours
walking through streets lit-up
by a warm light that was white and cold.
We discovered a new intimacy
as yet unknown to both of us.
Your gloved hand in mine
had begun to save my life.
Shining and dark, sixty years have gone by:
even in the hardest there was the heat
of those snowy streets.
This past year as well: when I, weakened
by chemo that has not succeeded
in curing me of this lymphoma,
have had you beside me with the same smile,
helping me to put together these poems.
I offer them to you as a year ends
that has been one of the happiest of my life.

The kitchen

The window, with its two panes of glass,
opens on to street level. In winter,
we keep the light on, those dark mornings,
and passers-by see us eating our breakfast.
Later, if it's fine, a ray of sun
writes a beautiful memory on the table:
that of the pair of us among other voices,
first when they were babies: then the two girls
and the boy, so many conversations and laughter.
You and I talking, as well,
in the kitchen at night, while they are asleep.
The fear of what might be coming
ended there when it arrived.
Those sunny mornings, peaceful nights,
as though they were still looking into our eyes.
Now there are no paths that come from there.
There are no paths, but we are not lost.

Museums

I have always found it tiring and boring
to look at altarpieces taken from churches,
paintings representing scenes from the Bible,
monarchs on horseback, sumptuous clothing
where the painter shows off in every fold,
keeping the beast covered-up. I like paintings
where I can gaze at men and women,
quite often poor, in their own worlds
of peaceful interiors, at work or at ease.
All-embracing and cruel, Brueghel's works,
the icy clarity of Flemish painting, liberate me.
The well-mannered disorder of the Impressionists,
and the thin women, shadowy and sad,
that Nonell painted.
The loneliness of Hopper, of Balthus and Freud,
of Paula Rego and Bacon. Maybe I shan't have time
to see them again, but they are inside me,
like the underwear folded away in the cupboard.

Silent woman

It has been hard to understand you:
I imagine you with sorrows, huge and deep
and with so few words. For a long time
your silence has been part of my own self!
You are silent and I talk. This is how we love.
The way we miss our daughter
is different as well. How to know, sometimes,
whether it's you or I in the coldest place?
I speak from a morning that has been strange.
You were coming out of the shower and I was going in,
holding on as I always do to the handrails
we installed for the girl's safety.
Beneath the water I wept and you, drying yourself,
said to me sadly: *Don't cry any more,*
we're so old we could never have looked after her.

The time has come in this affable song
To light a small fire in a field covered in hoar-frost.
And now, what shall we call all this?
It's fine to call it love. What else could we call it?
You and I are closer together than ever,
and, together, we're going farther away.
Like this glittering of the stars.

Ángel González, a memory

(for Luis García Montero)

A night in Madrid with friends.
For both of us, within the span of our lives,
it had become very late.
Seated and quiet, we said very little to each other.
Talking, friendship, were refinements
that were already starting to lose their significance.
In very few words you told me
that it was sadness
that gave your eyes their kind expression.
Your solace of long nights and drinking
and my rising at dawn to work on construction-sites
had never managed to meet up.

Don't talk about this with anybody

In the darkness of the small hours I sense behind me
the mountain of snuffed-out days
like smashed bottles, dark smithereens of glass
that no ray of light will ever penetrate.
I open the window a little
and see the rusty bowl –
the theatricality of the full moon –
like a message I hadn't counted on.
Raquel is asleep. I look at her and think:
don't talk about this with anyone but her.
When the only horizon with any meaning
suddenly crosses over into loneliness,
it means that the future is now. You and her.

From poverty

They were my earliest years, when my eyes opened
on a broad landscape of dry-farming.
I've never forgotten the marvellous moment
of clapping my hands at the water of the channel
when my grandfather, by raising the little sluice-gate,
allowed it to enter the field,
and flow along all the gullies made by the hoe.
Happiness comes to me from poverty.
Sometimes, in the broad but harsh
landscape of dry-farming that is my present age,
I sense the child's eyes questioning me,
smiling and trusting, asking if we are coming
to the place where I always told him we were going.

Clear and difficult

Behind the cruellest line a path awaits us.
The one reading it is surprised to find themselves smiling
at what had seemed so pitiless.

We always need to be able to open some door.
The poem is the key that the reader brings to his eyes.

Seductions, after so much time

The distant stars are the most beautiful
thanks to impassive forces
that hold them there in the night sky.
Without the strength with which,
ever since we were young,
we have confronted infidelity,
we would never have managed to feel
the tenderness of this old age.
Desire, mistrust and kindness
made it difficult. From those days
there remains only a memory made of silences.
What never comes back is the most painful.
But that is where the firmest
and most loyal part of our love took root.

Lost village

As though the brightness of the day
just beginning were irritating them,
the birds now shriek, rather than sing.
There is no one on the narrow road,
and when I come to the pond with its dark water
I feel it, sombre and sullen, watching me as I pass.

Facing me I have the hill with the houses clinging to it
where scarcely anyone now lives.
But if I had come here when I was a child
I would have seen lots of folk
coming out at this hour, with animals and tools,
to work in their fields.

This is the reason the water of the pond,
when I walk past it, looks so grim.
Because I have always spoken of the village and its crops
as *this landscape*. As though with the light of day,
and who knows if it's the same light irritating the birds,
I might give this name to a drama so remote
that it's beyond my understanding.

Wild Creature

Nor dread nor hope attend
A dying animal;
A man awaits his end
Dreading and hoping all;
Many times he died,
Many times rose again,
A great man in his pride
Confronting murderous men
Casts derision upon
Supersession of breath;
He knows death to the bone –
Man has created death.

W.B. YEATS, 'Death'

When it comes to death, I think that what Yeats wrote
is the most exact: that we have created it ourselves.
All this jumble of scythes and skeletons,
resurrections and paradises, is ours.
I am getting to know better and better
the inner wilderness where each ends up alone
and with one conviction:
understanding is the only ennobling thing.
But that has to have been in place from when young,
for this is the only way our intelligence
will succeed in saving us.

Because poetry, for the one writing it, is
learning to write one's self.
For the one reading it, it is learning to read one's self.
What is important about a poet is what they write.
And consolation comes to those who read with understanding.

Beloved time with her

The staircase is narrow, with high steps,
set between two walls with handrails.
I was then a young man, caught hold, sprang
upward and in a trice would reach the top.
While she, who didn't use her crutches at home,
would grasp a handrail in each hand and,
smiling, making a great effort, climb slowly.
Now that I have become just as weak,
I climb slowly and likewise with a smile.
Because there is an impetus from weakness.

Iliad

Agamemnon has imprisoned Chryseis, the daughter of the
old priest, Chryses, and refuses to accept the generous
ransom the distressed old man brings him, and turns him
out of doors with threats.

It's about the cruel, permanent urge
to dominate one another. It's the beginning.
Today there are millions, many millions,
who have died because of it, and violently.
Nothing of what we are has changed:
it always takes us back to the opening of the *Iliad*.
Chryses, the old father, loved his daughter:
as I love mine, and he does what I would do.
I recognise myself after three thousand years.

The only thing that has changed is the science:
not Agamemnon – and not even Pythagoras –
would be able to understand what we explained.
But it is not enough to halt disasters.
Who knows whether we will even miss the *Iliad*.
At least it takes place in a cleaner sea,
beneath a purer air, than we have ever known.
The rest is the same: atrocities, war.
Just as Homer, clearly and with understanding, tells it.

Note on truth

You will recognise it, but you have to make the effort
to search for it, which always takes time.
It consoles and persuades in an instant,
and it doesn't matter if it says terrible things,
such as the poem where Różewicz speaks
from a concentration camp:
The mother presses
a monster to her heart.
It's not what a prophet wrote in the sand
and afterwards erased.
Even a God cannot erase the truth.

Silence and survival

I am always silent, even when speaking
and do so even with tenderness and respect.
My own voice isolates me inside myself.
I do this so as not to listen: I disappear.
Without knowing what it is nor to what I owe the time,
I listen to it while it crosses this silence
that my voice protects so well.

First lesson

Living meant breathing through the thick scarf
while the stove was being lit early in the morning.
We children had the freedom
given to us by what was quite difficult for the elderly.
I grew up in the smallest space
there can be between order and disorder:
there is always this hole where everyone else
will forget about you. You just need to know
that the price of that will be loneliness.

Orpheus

It's happiness that moves me to write.
It always leaves its trace in one or two lines.
Fearing the cruelty of believers,
I have kept quiet about a lot of things, for example,
a long-standing aversion to fatherlands,
mine and that of others. In this way, when young,
I was able to survive the threats
from those followers of gods and ideologies,
the sheep of shepherds who have never existed.
Just for that, with an iron grip,
they lead the dark human flock
in order to hurl them over the cliffs.
Intimacy alone is a real space:
here is the place of safety from which to resist.
Don't ever leave your house again.

The calm of coming back

My youth was like that of a wolf
but certainly not the one in the song
that my romantic mother used to sing:
the one who fell in love with a star.

The past, from time to time,
out of some sad and very beautiful place,
sends me such a dazzling signal
that my eyes, all these years later, fill with tears.
I'm searching for tranquillity without any trace of epic.
I lay the table here, I do so under the light
of long-ago summers,
and am happy to feel myself darkening
like the vines after the grape-harvest.

A warm black air from the past
speaks to us of ourselves:
Raquel, you have loved a lonely man
who has now come too close
to the limit of himself, where mystery begins.
It's the end, Raquel: we're going home.

The poem and the wall

Beyond the horizon there rises a winter's day.
The poplar's black branches: the cold and rosy sun
has lit up the stone wall of the house.
It's an innocent and dangerous hour:
it must have been so too for those who made a fire
in caves that smelled of smoke,
excrement and slaughtered animals.
I think of a day –
hundreds of thousands of years ago –
and a brightness similar now to this.
In the bleakness of the cavern
there rose up, from the depths of a gaze,
the protective idea of the wall.
Someone, among the shadows,
was gazing at paintings or signs
made on the rock and lit by the fire.
The thought grew
like a great tree beneath the stars,
at the same time as there arose the warmth –
still far-off and indistinct – of the house.
Watching how the day is being born, I think,
gratefully, of architecture
and of the first people who could listen
to some hexameters from the *Odyssey*.
I have always kept faith with the poem and with the wall.

Depths of poverty

It will soon be dawn: in the bathroom
I look at the excessive whiteness of the toilet-bowl
and think of the innocence of water that carries away –
always making a noise – whatever it may be.
The body begins its resignation,
its creaturely resignation, while I realise
that what resembles the mind most closely
is the sewage network.
However much reason claims to speak only
about feelings and intelligence,
defecating and urinating are important.
There is something there
that comes from the Old Testament.

In the little village where I spent my childhood,
I was frightened of falling into the latrine
that gave on to the stable, now emptied of animals.
Later came Franco-ism and its lavatories
made of filthy china, with snippets of newspaper
hanging from a hook, a lot of cold.
It's all so distant. And yet it's only recently
that I have come to understand
what the night sky is always trying to tell us.
What the fox and blackbird know.
It dawns on me with a flash that inside us
the whole of the Old Testament is still stacked up.

Morning in Sant Just

A kindly sun caresses
the farmhouse courtyard. Some full tables
beneath the sheltering palm
and faces all around that are familiar to me.
But, in all of them, there is the trace of an absence:
each carries in their eyes someone no longer here.
I too know those I carry in my glance,
and I think of those who will welcome me
soon to their eyes. What will they end up seeing?
The trusting sparrows, pecking away,
foraging on the ground and below the empty tables.
Watching them, I know I always associate them
with that childhood poverty
which, pitilessly, always comes back at the end.

Family lunch

Eating lunch with an old man and the three women –
the young men had fled,
when the war ended, to France –
I gazed around me with interest.
In many homes, often hanging from the lamp
above the dining-room table, there would be
a fly-paper, broad and anointed with a shiny,
sweet and sticky paste. It would revolve
while it attracted the flies, that fell into the trap
and went on blackening it. You could hear
their death-throes, the buzzing of desperate wings
in a useless attempt to fly.
I was four years old and it fascinated me.
But today, I am puzzled to hear once again
that buzzing of dying flies.
Humanity, darkening the earth.

A simple farewell

Solitary people who gaze at the sea
or search for privacy deep inside a wood.
When I was young, I still admired
that romanticism, but I long ago
lost interest in grandeur.
I also used to endure the boredom
of the art, music and poetry
of the avant-garde, pathetic and banal,
and much more so as time goes on.
Now, at my age, sensing the end evokes for me
a simple, dark-green field of potatoes
blanketed in mist.
But gratitude prompts me to add
Winterreise – tenor and piano:
may Schubert accompany me!

The final intimacy

When I wash my hands I think how powerful
the symbolism of such a simple action can be.
Hands that love each other, working hands,
that are like you and me, and are almost
the same age as the years we've been together.
At the moment when one of us ceases to be present,
the other will start to feel in their hands
what they will, to all appearances, have lost.
While there are hands, we shall both be together.
The final intimacy, never imagined.

The beginning of everything

Each day, until the evening was far advanced,
we were without light. It was barely any time
since the Civil War had finally ended.
Two women were sewing, I played at their feet,
while all the time it was growing darker.
With a cry of joy all three of us greeted it,
when suddenly it came back, lighting up the room.
But what I was waiting for was the mystery
of the voices of the singers from the radio,
in spite of not fully grasping what they were saying.
In the night of that village,
I ended up falling asleep with my head beside the speaker,
sure that I was flying towards happiness.
Nor was I wrong: eighty years later,
I still sing to myself the songs
I heard on the radio,
and I fly, I fly through the same mystery
that protects me, from the time when I was a child.

Protections, consolations

Memories are becoming more and more muddled:
maybe we gradually become
one single memory, that's bigger but more vague,
an endearing but feeble protection,
as when mist wraps itself around your house.

I think that what I should search for
is another shelter, more solid and more free –
though without warmth, and sinister at times.
Because now it will have to be real,
no more substituting anything or anyone.
These are the last consolations: and also the hardest.

Rachid Boudjedra

It was during the long, cruel War
of Algerian Independence,
when we were students in Barcelona.
It's now a long time since they liberated themselves,
though not from their own violence.
Rachid is a writer, we have not met again.
Somewhere I read something he had said:
All revolutions end in failure,
but even so, they have to take place.

I imagine how the Algerians
are forgetting the country that he and I talked about.
With the army, who are still in control there,
they go on talking about revolution,
but there is none left from those who began it:
not one of those lads who, intent
on opening the frontier with Morocco,
saw the oldest fighter hurl himself
against the electric fence.
How sad to have to call for rejoicing
for something that has never existed.
It's what Sisyphus is thinking while he pushes
that hard and heavy rock up the mountain.
And goes on thinking it, when he gets to the top,
watching the rock go rolling down again.
Dear Rachid.

Faraway smiles

Lying awake beside you, staring into the dark,
I felt as though the children were still here
and sleeping, each in his or her room.
I don't know how long it lasted but, suddenly,
I felt such tenderness of an intensity
I had never known.

It begins to grow light.
I go through the empty rooms and gaze at
the clear eyes and trusting smiles
from the photographs in their frames.
Here the children are, for me, at once
smiles from far away – suddenly so close –
and also silences that come from some strangers
who must now be getting up in their houses.

Seagulls

I like to see them when they hang there
very high up and suspended, barely moving,
as though the future were watching over us.
In the empty blue of the air
our iron Iliad is coming to an end.
Nothing and no one will watch over us.
Absolute solitude is approaching,
the future the highest gulls are gazing at.

A price

Among my books I find the collection of poems
by Thomas Hardy: it's the one I used to read
while she would be listening seriously
to her music. We used to go to a café
on the Rambla on Sunday afternoons.
There is always something that reminds me
that I still have that young girl,
even though it's twenty years now
that she's been gone. Those cafés too.
The places where we sustain our life
are always the hardest because it's where
everything to do with love remains.

Chamber music

Lluís Claret and Anna Mora, Valldoreix

In the big concert-halls,
when a piece ends, while I still hear it,
familiar and at the same time so far away –
there are a few moments, mine alone,
when the silence matters.
But thousands of hands start clapping,
there's even the odd shout.
Suddenly it's like having fallen into a trap.

I prefer to be here, in the little sitting-room.
Cello, piano, a few friends.
Let a sonata move slowly on
while, through the window, afternoon darkens.
I find it difficult to listen
among a crowd. I often lose myself
in the forest of my own nostalgias.
That is why so many centuries have not been able
to erase that name: *chamber music*.

Love and fear

When we were young, in the first flat we had,
what security there was in that gesture
of never locking the door.
In this way, almost forty years went by.
But when we began to feel
old age approaching, we suffered a loss
that left us forever heartbroken.

From the first moment, you and I independently,
without having spoken about it even once,
both locked the house every night.
What sudden fear do we have to confront?
With so much time already gone by, whom or what
does the gentle, powerful gesture
of turning the key in the lock replace?
The firmest and deepest foundation
of our happiness is ignorance.
Not knowing to what new misfortune
we are coming close and making our way.

The long ending

Remembering Joan Marsé

In some godforsaken passageway
or in some unknown room,
the white colour that hospitals wear
reveals its dark background. It's like the night sky
that is slowly bringing closer and closer to him
the fiery spirals that caused us to invent
the gods and hope.
Now, each novel out of all those he has written
is jumbled up in a vague remembering,
and out of this there rises this smile
that is lucid but at the same time unaware
in a way he would never have been able to imagine.

His generation, that was at one and the same time
such a literary one
and so joyful in such a sad country,
was covered-up by abandonment,
as detritus covers the bottom of the sea.
Now he, who was the most kind-hearted –
and he is the last one to go – does so after
all the characters in his novels have walked away.
He smiles because he too lived in barbarism,
in the very same place, together with all of them.

In the early morning

I have turned off my light and lain down.
You go on reading beside me.
What I'm doing is turning my back on the world,
but I know that where I am gazing
we will end up going with bare feet:
these feet of ours that have searched for each other
beneath the sheets for such a long time.
There is no gesture as warm as this.
You and I, reading in bed early in the morning,
we're like the headlights on the *deux chevaux*
that used to carry us along tiny roads
in a world without motorways, where we had to
stop for the night when going to Paris.

What is approaching?

Somewhere behind my gaze
is a theatre that no one ever enters now
and where, without words, the same play
is always being staged. I don't know
who wrote it, but here is where it comes
and is out of danger, this drive of mine.
Nearly a thousand full moons have shone,
radiant in a sky of sumptuous black
or else concealed behind banks of cloud
that have sailed past my windows.
The most frightening ones begin to arrive,
those of truth: the most secret moons
of one's own sad indignity.
I cannot create the poem: I have to search for it
locked up in the gloomiest prisons
that life has been leaving behind inside me.

The picture of Santes Creus monastery

Well-drawn, painted in watercolour, with no people in it,
my father drew it when he was a student.
I've always seen it at home: the square in the foreground,
the statue of the bishop above the fountain
(being a left-wing student he left his mitre off)
and in the background the monastery, its austere wall
of pink stone with the closed gateway.

The war began almost immediately.
The blue sky of the drawing with no one in it
and so many thousands of dead, as young as my father,
and still lying in fields and ditches,
mean that I may never forget why I have loved
neither this country nor this land.
And because, in spite of it all, I have never left it:
I could never know another place as completely as I know this,
and nothing protects like knowledge.

Autumn in Elizondo

(for Ramon and Lola)

The rain and the grey light make the calm,
russet foliage of the beeches shine.
With their beauty they are trying
to affirm that perhaps trees think.
That if we one day end up losing our fear,
we would be like the red beech wood I am gazing at.
For me, a tree is a quiet mystery.
And I sense I would like to die in a place
where I could see woods like these
which, from their roots to their branches,
are a message of some peace I know nothing of.

Final pause

In bed in the darkness, faces you have loved
draw near, some nights: you don't want to let them go.
Make it so that they live inside your poems:
you still have to write the most difficult ones,
like the late sonatas by Haydn and Beethoven.
It's an incorruptible austerity
that the end calls for. Be quiet and listen.
That's what you called love, in a line you wrote.

Murmur of rain

Don't leave anything on your plate: it should look
as though no one has eaten off it:
this is what they said to me when I was a child.
Everything is fleeting, simple, but also profound.
Pain has no bottom: neither does being a victim
presuppose any kind of goodness.
But it soothes and it moves me
to recall those very humble days.
The gap where the past smiles at us is so narrow:
the crack in a not-quite-closed door.
No: do what you will, there's nothing left on the plate.
It's always as though no one has eaten off it.

The house

It protects us and keeps what we have been.
Things no one will ever find:
ceilings where we have left grievous glances,
voices that have lingered, silenced, in the walls.
The house organises its future forgetting.
Suddenly, a draught, and a door
slams shut with a hard sound like a warning.
Each one of us is their house, the one they have built.
And which in the end is empty.

Consolations

The oldest is solitude:
the effort a child makes to become that.
And so I discovered, in the depths of happiness,
what harshness there needs to be in it.
Because of all that, those years were the most free.
And at sixteen, there came the unforgettable:
discovering the ocean and contemplating in it
the green and majestic island, spread out around
the highest, snowy peak, that was the volcano.
One moonless night, while all at home were sleeping,
and my lamp switched off, I leaned on my elbows
at the open window. With my face to the horizon
I knew that I was looking towards the ocean,
but I didn't know what it was of myself
I was searching for in the darkness of the sea.
For the first time I sensed
that the future existed, that, without seeing it,
I was gazing out at it. And the ocean stretched
for thousands of blue miles around
the white ocean-liners, decommissioned
so many, many years ago now.
The lost world from which my poems
still come, even this one.

Building

Building a house well means talking
affectionately to people
whom you'll never meet. As with passion,
when faults appear in a building
you have always to ask yourself
whether it's better to reinforce or to knock it down
and start from scratch.
Reinforcing can sometimes be alarming, and is harder.
The only thing we know how to do is move forward,
our food is hope.
This is the mystery of a failure.

Nightfall for old lovers

Figures begin to look sombre through the glass,
dark trees with abandoned nests
like the faces and voices that linger
among the carcasses of a lost past.
This tends to be our time for listening to a concert:
sometimes in pyjamas and dressing-gown,
sitting and gazing at the Rambla in that picture
I used to look at when I was young and living at home.
So many years now that it's here with you and me, Raquel,
hanging in the sitting-room: the Barcelona
of when we met. The mystery of back then.

The only loyalty

That obstinate boy who searched
for so many sunsets, today no longer needs
to be loyal to any kind of beauty.
This is now my twilight,
but I cannot abandon life, shining
like a star in the midst of darkness.
You and I drag behind us – each in the disguise
of some passion, the mistakes of youth.
At our age, what can they matter to anyone?
I at your side, Raquel, and you at mine,
we have always been true to each other's pain.

Coming out of a concert

(for Cristina Liso, from Pamplona to Áriz)

She has been listening to Symphony
number three, the *Eroica*. She found it over-long,
with military echoes and somewhat bombastic.
This sensible and even-tempered elderly woman
goes home at night, attended
by a certain sadness.
Eighty years have now gone by since the Civil War
and she has been bored by concepts such as *Spain*,
the word *enemy* and its old dishonesty.
She never discusses it with anyone,
but she thinks that some day we'll go back to killing each other.
This is what she heard said, when just a little girl, at home.
Going along in her car, she plans to avoid
concerts and symphonies that are over-grandiloquent,
like this Beethoven today, across which
Napoleon gallops violently on horseback.

And all at once she smiles:
in her house, among the fields,
she has so much music to listen to.
As she thinks of the *Nocturnes* she will put on
tomorrow when the sun rises beyond the windows,
the night meanwhile is changing: it has changed
when suddenly, getting out of the car,
she lifts her head and finds once more the stars.

Dark Night of the Soul

...my house now being quiet and still

ST JOHN OF THE CROSS

I think of the poor rats that we hate
because they resemble all of us too closely.
Both they and we end up as nothing
more than a few handfuls of dust
which is what remains of the dumb, huge
and distant light from which we have come.
Yet only time can ensure that living
may mean each time more truth,
though it may be at a very high, hard price.
That may be the most honest thing awaiting us
when we enter old age: it depends
on how dark our spirit may be.
And here intuition ends:
I affirm that never more
will my mind let me return
to places I thought to go and which did not exist.
And which, all at once, put to shame
my own rat-like solitude.

Deep paradox

In your gaze there is the dark gold
of so many distant summers.
In mine, Raquel, there are the ploughed fields
of a winter that no one will sow.
I sense my thoughts settling then rising up again,
like flocks of sparrows searching for food.
Existence is like an ivy-bush
that with its own strength splits the wall
while it adorns and hides it for us in leafy greenness.
This is where love has endured until now,
although its fate has been
so entwined with the fate of a ruin.

Two encounters

They were a surprise in the monotony
of a morning in some classroom, and I felt
that blazing inrush into an unknown place.
One master showed me the meaning
that words had. Another brought me close
to my first poet: I go on reading him.

The two flashes of lightning in my apprenticeship
have ended up casting the rest of my time
spent in classrooms into darkness.
Now, what is left of adolescence
are years of oblivion and obscurity for me:
three times the length of time needed
in order to read those stories that were then unknown
to me, with the unforgettable, mysterious
and beautiful name of the *Thousand and One Nights*.
With just a few flashes of lightning, the mind is lit up.
For an old man the rest has no meaning.

A poignant indifference

I was thinking that I still had time
to understand the profound meaning
of ceasing to exist. I was comparing it
with disinterestedness, oblivion, deep sleep,
the houses where we'd lived and never gone back to.
I thought that I was understanding it,
that I was gradually freeing myself of the enigma.
But I was still a long way from knowing
that I am not freeing myself. It is death that is freeing me:
it allows me indifferently,
to come close to some truth.
Inexplicably, I find this moving.

Everything is going quiet

When I was young, I firmly believed
that being serene allows you to imagine.
I now know that there in the imagined life,
the worst of me has its foundation.
I have forgotten so many historic versions:
the lies of the classics and the romantics.
And then, how tedious the present labyrinth is,
so ugly and complex all at once.
Wrapped round it all, a starry night
I will never be able to understand.
Today the only thing that speaks to me is a voice
rising up out of the hardness of life itself,
the only one in which I find some truth:
music, covering nothingness with beauty,
poems I have written,
the strength of love and the word together.
You and I. Those who may read them
from their own solitude.

Mistakes and sewers

Memories are gradually losing their force.
But you and I are together: you're here now,
as intelligent and full of laughter as always.
This is the only love that we talked about so much
without knowing anything about it, while we searched
in other beds for who knows what of non-existent sex
where lovers cease and end up hurling themselves
from the ruins of romantic mistakes.
They are among the sewers that the Enlightenment
brought into broad daylight, claiming to be the purest
and deepest waters of what my grandmother
always called *this vale of tears.*

Inspiration

I sense her in the darkness, just before I fall asleep:
when she comes, she stays a few moments, then suddenly goes.
Each one of us has his or her night,
their own night with something
that never comes.
But I need this strength:
even if winter – capable at one and the same time
of the most terrible siege and the loveliest landscape –
were now saying to me with its tired gesture: enough,
you are now a snowy field unmarked by footprints.

I love that young man who began to write,
like a son. I sense him beside me
accompanying this humble
presocratic poet I would like
to have become in my old age.

Gratitude

(for Mònica and Carles)

How to know what you have been,
you, from the girl who was always
taking on the world, and capable
of laughing and crying all at once.
And you, from the child who learned to love us
with fear in your eyes and discovering music.
But there was also the difficult tenderness
of looking after your sister at home.
Until you both grew up and went away,
between us all we gave her a life.
When she was thirty she died: she never knew
how much she gave us and what she took from you.
I often think of her and of you
and I humbly ask of you one hope.
Today it's all long gone. But pain comes back
like a nocturnal bird, crossing in front of the moon.
I don't care what death may be:
I don't know if it's a good guess.
But I know we're not dealing with a mistake.

Reasons and ways

I value what's real: iron when it was being forged
into a nail or a plough, any feeling that I
can recognise in a clean and clear shape.
But I'm also fascinated to understand what it means
for me to become quite soon oblivion in the shape
of a handful of dust inside a galaxy.
Meanwhile, I don't know what the future is.
Perhaps it's a memory: it could be my own,
that rises and flies strongly towards some place.

Betrayal is no longer possible

(for Antonio and for José)

I don't feel capable now of paying attention
to the labyrinths of philosophy,
nor, likewise, to the disorder
coming to me, and unstoppable, from physics.
The only treasure I have left
is feeling how our eyes are becoming
at the same time kinder and more calm.
Often, I hear this wind howling
out of places of the past.
I listen to it without anxiety:
it tells me that betrayal is no longer possible.

Walking through a forest at night

The path goes onward beneath the trees
and through clearings beneath the starry sky.
When I was young I gazed at everything
as that solitary, romantic character does
who, with a staff contemplates the sea of clouds,
standing on rocks and turning his back on us.
One day I realised that in gazing
I would see little: that now it was all about
walking with my eyes shut, imagining
all these other darknesses that there are
inside these crumbs of soil I trample on,
or else inside one hair or in the mind.
All around are these dark places where
elementary particles spin in the same silence
as constellations, stars and galaxies.
It is what we ourselves are, not words,
or intelligence or feelings:
a very tiny part of that immense night.
Nothing to do with life, but with one aspect,
the most pretentious and impoverished, of death.

A joyous prudence

(Sonata for cello and piano in A major by César Franck)

There is so much that I have been ignorant of and have lost.
And, on the other hand, how am I saved by the powerful sound
of Jacqueline du Pré, the cellist
who died so young.
Each is the soloist of their own silence:
they have to be well aware of when to come in.
Maybe I am a rat that pain
has hardened and who, one spring morning,
stopped to listen to the birds singing.

Building work

At once it became the house for summer holidays,
winter holidays, and for weekends,
always full of the children, later the grandchildren.
A house made of stone on three floors
surrounded by ploughed fields, mist and rain.
But for years now we've been coming on our own.
And now work begins so we can live on the ground floor,
beside the lawn and the rose bushes.

It's the last time I'll work as an architect,
and it will be for you, who will one day come alone
and think of me while listening to the birds.
I picture you in summer, when the sun comes out
with the doors open on to the garden
while in the fields someone will be reaping.
And – like you and me, we've always done so at this time –
you put on some Mozart.

Under a deep blue sky

A stone wall, a thought or a star:
there is nothing that has not been immersed in time,
which is this quiet, invisible presence,
that makes everything come to be ever more distant.
But I sense a more complex assumption
behind time. It's a darkness
that is there at the back of the mind, a gloomy alley
with a truth I don't know what to call,
because it does not even have a name.
And to understand it is even more difficult.
Impossible and distant.
I have only one clue, that is your tenderness,
and only one first step, which is you. Nothing else.

Sick old man

In the darkness inside me, but silent,
there is a storm of wind and rain
and not much time for understanding.
There begins a defence that is merciless:
death knows only one feeling:
that of indifference. As for me,
what dominates – still powerful,
violent, almost – is the desire to live.
To live though the sickness may be ferocious and hoarse:
a darkness that speaks to me of a winter
which, arriving in summer, has been colder than ever.
I have spent it huddled in a woollen jersey,
my legs wrapped in a blanket
and shivering with cold, with little strength.
My eyes facing the light but, inside,
deeper with every passing day, blackness
and at the same time, and powerful, happiness.

About Babel

What harm could it do to create a city –
the only one, the first, and at its centre that tower?
The Bible doesn't make it clear: what it says
is that we were about to build
something serious for the first time.
The malice of that god is the only really clear thing
in the story of Babel: he chopped up language
into thousands of other languages. It is so sad to think
that the mother tongue has a merit that is ours alone,
and that these thousands of languages are a wealth.

There is where our downfall began,
or else where there appeared, instead of the gods,
some new, human intelligence
which I have lived beside for over eighty years.
Maybe the age of Babel is now ended
and ours has begun, dependent
only on that force
that holds up the night sky around me
and those I love. Well-protected and, at the same time,
sheltered from the worst, which is nothingness.

Josep Maria Subirachs
(1927-2014)

(to the children, who years ago ceased to be so:
Roger, Judit, Mònica and Dani)

I am thinking of you while I contemplate
the portrait of Raquel, serious, pensive,
that you painted when she was young. Where her gaze
has that intelligence of then and of today.
Any sculpture or drawing of yours
makes me go back to those fifty years of friendship,
to the memories of dinners at your house,
you and Cecília, Raquel and I
with the children's laughter,
around the kitchen table.

Later, the sculptures
ploughed the difficult sea of that Barcelona
in a monstrous ship of stone –
the Sagrada Família with its masts –
flagship of those streets
in the poor part of the Eixample district.
Deeply moved, I watched how you forged
the great bronze doors:
I still open them in memory
so as to enter again the world of those mornings:
the pair of us in your studio,
in front of a row of etchings
and talking about sculpture, drawing and poetry.
The safe refuge of our friendship.

A daughter

The years pass fruitlessly if it's about
appeasing the pain of having lost you.
The only desire that is left is the honesty
of not being able to stop weeping for you.
And of not having forgotten that precise instant,
as when a gust of wind cuts off the flame
and bears it off through the air to snuff out the candle.
Is it you who are far from me or I from you?
It's starting to be many years since I began to feel –
like the slight sound a leaf makes, falling –
the particular nostalgia of a world
I might be able to love for its beauty.
I am struggling to say: I don't know where you can be.
And let my heart not break,
knowing the reason why you are not here.

Vincent Van Gogh

He must have known it: of the real world,
the most difficult truth to understand,
is that life ends with simplicity.
Because nothing exists outside the real world.
A tree, a mountain, silence and rain,
are forever true. They have no need
of such turgid stuff as theories,
a pretentious world that believes that death –
which means no more than that a life is ending –
is a final and transcendent truth.
Painter of firmaments, clogs, beds, chairs,
and fields of wheat that crows fly over,
Vincent Van Gogh did not let himself be fooled.

With you

We were very young. Immediately
there began a long spell of misfortunes and losses
out of which the children themselves were making
the radiant memory that goes on saving us.
Having crossed these winters of ours,
we smile at grief, that has become old.
Nor are we wary of being sad:
today it all forms part of the same strength.

In spite of the sufferings that made me solitary,
wherever it may be that I arrive when it grows dark,
I have never felt less afraid of this road.
You, together with poetry,
for twenty years now, are all I have.
It is the best ending. Before dawn
I have woken up and I start to read
what I wrote before going to sleep:
of what use will it be? It may be that poetry,
which arrived one day when I was a boy,
will leave when it has to. That will be the moment,
with you and with indifference, for no longer remembering.

The forgotten dream

It was the night of my fourth birthday.
A tall man, dressed in a single garment
of white woollen underwear
from his neck to his ankles,
rose up before me near the burning hearth.
Through the window I could see a dark sky with no stars.
It looked like my past, which didn't yet exist.
A warm house at bedtime
and out there, in the darkness, that war.
For me, time and its lies were just beginning:
faster and faster every day, with no trace of subtlety,
indifferent and always accelerating
yet surrounded by the deepest silence.

All at once, deliberately, I direct my gaze forwards:
eighty years have passed that I can't find any trace of,
and I meet a window as black as that one,
and a warm house in an icier winter.
Very early I see young people going to work,
taking children to school. They leave their houses in darkness.
I have been their age, and now it's as though
it lasted just a few moments, but leaving me
with an enduring respect for all that is complex.

Attempt at conclusions

Now and again I remember houses I have lived in:
who can be living there now,
and the time when I was there, where is it now?
But we cannot keep time anywhere,
it too disappears: first we lose the present,
then, little by little, memory starts to go.
And following its rhythm, we also lose the future.

This is why, ever since I was young,
I have distanced myself from the muddle of religion,
wanting no part of it in my life.
I love what is real, because that is what my non-being
will also be when it becomes oblivion,
and possibly energy in some black hole.

For all I know I belong to a terrible universe
that deceives me as it reveals itself to me
in the night-sky, so remote and so calm.

Courtyard song

It is beginning to rain very slowly.
You and I, in the shelter of the porch,
listen to the drops beating,
as though following a partitura,
on the ivy leaves and on the large, serious,
classical foliage of the aspidistras.
But that is not what I was wanting
to say in these lines,
though it may all belong to the same story.

For the first time, like a truth,
I have felt that my time was now coming to an end.
We cannot forget what a brutal mix
of the toughest happiness and limitless sadness
our life has been.
Today, just like this porch, we are still real:
two old people who are talking
in this green courtyard while listening to the rain.
But now the only one able to hear them
will be he who one day reads this poem.

The past, so difficult at times

I am frightened of not understanding it.
This is where the real pain lies. It's not knowing
why I've lived for so long watching those I loved
die. The past holds a mystery
that resembles the one the full moon holds
when hanging in the night; it's as though I were seeing
how, in my solitude, they merge –
the old man who is happy to have been alive
and the young child who grew up amid the terror
of a Civil War that everyone has forgotten.
But you need to remember if you want to understand.
To understand even the icy presence
of the moon in the night and its theatre.

I was not aware of being so old.
Desolation has overwhelmed me:
we aren't careful enough, and we even believe
that wisdom and old age go together
in a world that is full of stupid old men.
It's only by not losing sight of pain
or of the silent, indifferent passage of time,
that we can attain a modicum of peace.
I am re-reading the *Iliad* and also the history
of the Civil War: the only difference
is that, three thousand years ago, in order to kill
they had only spears and swords. The beauty
of Homer and his hexameters
for the assassins of Greece. The icy realism
of Anthony Beevor's writing for the other killers,
the ones I had near me in childhood.

Another happy world

(the 1960s)

An island: Ibiza. We arrived at dawn
on a small cargo ship with a single crane
that deposited
our *deux chevaux* on the quayside.
There were you, me and our three-year-old daughter
on a huge beach, luxuriant with wild olive,
where so much emptiness made us afraid.

Paris, at the Café Flore talking with Alberti
with a mane of white hair and the Civil War,
savage and relentless, in the depths of his bright eyes.

An attic, our first home.
With a bed and, on either side, two chairs.
We didn't need other furniture:
the love we were beginning was just one-year-old.

You, me, and music

We discovered it together. The poetry
of Verlaine, of Rimbaud and Baudelaire
sung by Ferré, rang out on the record-player,
in a modest attic when Barcelona
wore the dreariness of that dictatorship
but at the same time the happiness
that our youth bestowed upon it.
We owe so much to the French *chanson*,
the one from the sixties, twentieth-century.
Montand sang us poems by Prévert:
Les feuilles mortes and *Barbara*.
We loved each other so much: and it all seemed
as though it would never become difficult.
We were still lacking loss and death.
And, as we gradually ceased to be young,
how much more did we come to need
Bach, Beethoven and Schubert: the mysterious
hardness, without words,
that music has, this consolation
that never needs to lose the trace of pain
while what goes on rescuing us is beauty.

Memory of a field

It was an ancient vineyard at the foot of a long bank
covered in a wilderness of bramble and thorn.
When we cleared it, it revealed –
standing tall and sturdy – a drystone wall.
It radiated truth and beauty,
like a well-made poem,
because, to say what you know, you need a few years:
to wait until memories merge
with our own selves.
Like that very strong drystone wall,
we need time to consolidate.
That's when being old has some advantages:
we can be strong and clear, just like the wall,
with nothing to hide us from the wind and the sun's rays,
and not ignoring death, which would mean not having
          understood life.

Fear of what we are

The crowd is always on the side of violence.
But it's solitude that is considered to be a punishment:
it frightens so many people. And yet the monster is
always in the crowd: among the demonstrators
or the police force, the big political meetings,
packed stadiums, marches with weapons,
armies attacking or defending themselves,
the heaped-up dead, the houses razed to the ground.
Why, then, this fear of solitude?
I find this species ruthless
of which I am a part. No other is so wicked.
It deceives when it is weak, when it shows us
the sufferings of children, of the old or sick.
But crowds need to kill.
Now that I'm very old and my insides are cold,
I would like to have been born a wild creature.

Our dead, Raquel

Our parents died – yours and mine –
fifteen or twenty years ago now, and still
we remember their youthful love affairs,
the war, the prisons, the escapes into France.
But there were younger dead too:
Marta – the sister whose death left you on your own –
and later – when she was thirty – our daughter.
While we were still a fairly young man and woman,
we believed that we lit up that darkness
by facing it with all the life we had in such abundance

But now we have reached a time with the certainty
that the silence and darkness – with stars or without –
are the beginning and the end of life.
It is a time where no consolation comes
behind words like dreams and hopes:
consolation comes from a stark calm
that rises from loving an entire life.
Since I have become old, I feel that for our dead
an intimate peace is shedding light on them.
So they welcome us.

One winter morning, 2020

Abandoned as a hopeless case by the doctors,
I listened to Tchaikovsky's piano concerto,
in which I'd been able to discern for the first time,
when I was very young, the power of music.

Talking to someone about weighty matters
is difficult for us, because these things
are to do with solitude.
Often, if this occurs, it's because we're moving
between closed doors and meaningless smiles,
words trudging through a desert.
Deceit and its silence – relentless –
has at times more force than music.
Then all that remains for us is the terror
of an instrument left lying on a chair
like an image of our death.

But often music triumphs:
uncertainty can prove to be far more profound
and better company than reassurance.

The highest mountain

(for Mariona, Mònica and Carles, for Eduard and Pol)

Wild creatures, we search for it,
even though we're always reluctant
to look up too far.
I don't know any answers that inspire me with confidence,
but it's thinking about it that is always meaningful.
From here I write today, protected and surrounded
by so much time together. I will go away loving you.
And something of me will try to come back.

EPILOGUE

A moment has come when I need
to imagine what will not happen next.
I'm talking about that ancient, dangerous force
that clearly grasps where you are going
and doesn't care that it may be useless.
I send out a cry directed at myself
like a last opportunity.
To smile at a ridiculous place while fearing nothing
and without distinguishing between truth and falsehood,
but to do it with the force that truth has
that it has never claimed to be. And which it isn't.
A force that many of us will have been aware of,
like a storm beating against the rocks,
and which I carry inside me
like the sea gone calm inside a cave
from which the noise of the storm can be heard.
A time I want to go back to when my shadow,
the one I had as a child, comes back to take my hand,
when that well-known moment comes.
That is the closest to a truth
and also the furthest from a lie
that my solitude can make use of.